SANDWICH RECIPE COOKBOOK

+50 Surefire Recipes for Making Panini

Adriana **Phillips**

TABLE OF CONTENTS

INTRODUCTION...5

PESTOTRAMEZZINI WITH ROCKET 7

PANINI WITH TOMATO AND MOZZARELLA 9

PANINI WITH HAM AND CHEESE 11

PANINI WITH CHICKEN..13

LEMON CHICKEN SANDWICH....................................15

COS PITA BREAD BAG 17

CLASSIC SMORES..19

CHEESE AND ARUGULA CORE SANDWICH.................21

CHEESE AND CUCUMBER SANDWICH 23

HOT SANDWICH WITH HAM AND EGG.......................25

QUICK SPRING SANDWICH...27

CREAM CHEESE BAGUETTES WITH RADISHES.......29

FETA AND BÜNDNERFLEISCH SANDWICH WITH ROCKET...31

EGG AND BAGUETTE SANDWICH...............................33

BROCCOLI HAM BREAD SLICES...................................35

WHOLE GRAIN TOAST...37

BAGUETTE WITH STRIPS OF CHICKEN.....................38

WILD GARLIC AND CHEESE SAUCE............................40

EGGPLANT SANDWICHES...42

APERITIF TOAST SQUARES...44

CIABATTA PANINI 46

AMERICAN DRESSING 48

DONER KEBAB..50

SAVORY SANDWICH CAKE 53

ENGLISH AFTERNOON TEA SANDWICHES...............56

PARTY PRETZEL..58

HUNTERBUN...60

PORK FILLET IN FLATBREAD WITH POINTED
CABBAGE AND GARLIC MAYONNAISE 62

VIP CLUB SANDWICH...65

CUCUMBER SANDWICH.......................................67

SANDWICH LASAGNA 69

AVOCADO SANDWICH 71

VEGETABLE SANDWICH 73

LEMON CHICKEN SANDWICH...............................75

CUCUMBER SANDWICH WITH LEMON BUTTER.......77

AMERICAN STEAK TOAST...................................79

WHOLE GRAIN HEALTHY SANDWICH 81

ITALIAN SANDWICHES..83

HAM SANDWICH 85

CLUB SANDWICH...87

GRILLED CHEESE SANDWICH..............................89

SHEEP CHEESE SANDWICH 91

AVOCADO SANDWICH CREAM...93

BANANA SANDWICH...95

CAMEMBERT SANDWICH 96

CUCUMBER SANDWICH...98

SNACK SANDWICH..99

WHOLE GRAIN BREAD WITH CURD CHEESE........... 101

FLANK STEAK SANDWICH...102

SHORTBREAD SANDWICH...105

CONCLUSION 106

INTRODUCTION

Well, as the name suggests, it's based on Make a Meal Where the Sandwich is Plato Main. So we take a meal in the form of a sandwich and alternate it with balanced and healthy dishes. Therefore, both vegetables and white meat or fish are available to lose a few pounds. Remember that no just any sandwich is served as we have to choose the seed bread or the whole grain and as natural as possible. So let's forget about sliced bread. In addition, the sandwich in question should be small and no longer than eight inches.

HEALTHY BREAKFAST

How Much Do You Lose in the First Week of the Diet?

If things go well, the sandwich diet can shed you 5 pounds a month. Because thanks to the variety of sandwiches, you will not be afraid to prepare an additional snack. Something basic that sometimes happens to us when we are on very extreme diets. So you can lose anywhere from 1 pound or 1.5 pounds each week. Of course, not all bodies are created equal and therefore there is even more to lose. Remember that in addition to diet, you should drink plenty of water and of course forget about any pre-cooked foods, fried foods, or pastries that often tempt us.

SANDWICH DIET MENU

Breakfast

Glass of coffee with skimmed milk, two slices of bread with light jam and a piece of fruit. You can alternate with a skimmed yogurt and fruit. This can be kiwi, pineapple, pear or tangerine as well as oranges.

Morning and afternoon

You can have a fruit or a natural yogurt. But you can also add infusions or coffee without sugar. If you're hungry, you can have more fruit and even add some veggies like carrots or tomatoes.

Food

This is where our sandwich arrives. Always whole grain bread or with seeds. We always make the sandwich with green leaves like lettuce or Swiss chard and rocket. In addition to these vegetables, they must contain that part of the protein that comes in the form of turkey or chicken. You can choose slices or grilled. Cream cheese, roasted peppers, boiled egg, ham, or even mussels. What do you like sandwiches For dessert you can have another fruit.

PESTOTRAMEZZINI WITH ROCKET

Servings:1

INGREDIENTS

- 2 TL Basil pesto
- 50 G Mozzarella
- 1 Cup Extra virgin olive oil
- 1 shot pepper from the grinder
- 1 Federation arugula
- 1 Schb   Sandwich bread
- 1 Pc   Tomatoes, big, ripe

PREPARATION

The bread is debarked and coated with basil pesto.
Mozzarella is cut into slices. Olive oil is put in a bowl, a
little salted, peppered and the mozzaralla slices are

dipped in it. The tomato is washed, peeled and cut into slices. The tomato slices are a little salted and peppered.

The bread is cut diagonally and one half is covered with tomato slices, the other half with mozzarella slices. Rocket is washed, shaken dry and put on the rolls. The second half of the bread is placed on top and lightly pressed.

PANINI WITH TOMATO AND MOZZARELLA

Servings:4

INGREDIENTS

- 4 Pc Ciabatta rolls or other white bread
- 150 G Mozzarella
- 80 G Parmesan, grated
- 1 prize   pepper
- 2 Stg sage
- 1 prize   salt
- 4 Pc tomatoes

PREPARATION

The fresh tomatoes are washed, quartered and cut into fine slices. Drain the fresh mozzarella and cut into bite-sized pieces. Wash the fresh sage, shake it dry and chop it finely.

Now mix the prepared ingredients with the grated Parmesan in a bowl and season well with salt and pepper.

Now cut the rolls open so that you can open them. Then the prepared filling can be evenly distributed over the rolls.

Close the rolls and roast them in the hot sandwich maker for about 3-5 minutes until crispy. Immediately serve the finished panini with tomato and mozzarella hot.

PANINI WITH HAM AND CHEESE

Servings:2

INGREDIENTS

- 4 Tbsp   butter
- 4 Schb   cheese
- 4 Schb   ham
- 8 Schb   Toast, panini or baguette
- 1 Pc   tomato

PREPARATION

Brush the toast slices from one side with a little fresh butter.

Now place a slice of ham and cheese on 4 slices of toast and cover each with a loose slice of toast. Wash and thinly slice the tomato and place on the topping.

Finally, place the panini with ham and cheese in the hot sandwich toaster and toast for about 3-5 minutes until golden brown and crispy.

PANINI WITH CHICKEN

Servings:2

INGREDIENTS

- 2 Pc Eggs
- 2 Tbsp mixed herbs
- 2 Pc Chicken breast fillets
- 200 ml oil
- 2 Pc Panini bread or ciabatta
- 1 prize pepper
- 4 Pc Lettuce leaves
- 1 prize salt
- 2 TL mustard
- 2 Pc tomatoes
- 2 TL Lemon juice

PREPARATION

For the panini with chicken, first season the chicken fillets well on both sides with salt and pepper. Fry these in a pan with a little oil on both sides for a few minutes until golden brown. Then take it out of the pan and cut into thin slices.

Now separate the eggs for the sauce and whisk the egg yolks with the lemon juice and mustard in a bowl. Then the oil is slowly poured in, stirring constantly, until it has a creamy consistency. Refine the sauce with the mayonnaise and season with salt, pepper and herbs.

Then cut open the Panini, spread the sauce and cover with the washed lettuce leaves. Wash the tomatoes, cut them into slices and also place them in the Panini. Now place the chicken slices on top and cover with the second slice of bread.

Finally, roast the Paninis in a hot Panini grill for about 4 - 5 minutes until crispy.

LEMON CHICKEN SANDWICH

Servings:2

INGREDIENTS

- 2 Pc Chicken breasts / chicken fillet
- 2 Tbsp   Flour
- 2 Tbsp   olive oil
- 1 Pc   Red peppers
- 1 Pc   Head of lettuce
- 1 prize   salt and pepper
- 8 Schb   Sandwich bread
- 0.5 Tbsp crushed fennel seeds
- 2 Tbsp   Lemon juice

PREPARATION

Wash the chicken breasts, pat dry and pat a little flat.
Pour the lemon juice over them and marinate for at
least 20 minutes.

Now mix the fennel seeds, flour, salt and pepper. Pat the chicken fillets dry and rub the spice mixture on them.

Heat the oil in a pan and fry the meat in it for about 20 minutes until it's done, then remove it from the pan.

Prepare the peppers and cut into strips. Put some oil in the pan and sauté the pepper strips in it. Add the lemon juice to the marinade and cook until it has evaporated. Wash the cucumber and cut it into slices.

Next, toast the sandwich breads and slice the chicken.

Place the chicken slices on a toast slice, pour the pepperoni and cucumber slices over them, cover with washed lettuce leaves and cover with another slice of toast.

COS PITA BREAD BAG

Servings:2

INGREDIENTS

- 2 Pc   Baby lettuce
- 1 Tbsp   butter
- 1 Tbsp   Butter for greasing
- 1 prize   Chilli flakes
- 4 Pc   ready-made pita breads
- 200 G Raclette cheese
- 1 prize   Salt pepper

PREPARATION

Remove the outer leaves from the lettuce (or other lettuce), wash the rest and cut into strips (put some fresh lettuce leaves aside). Butter a small baking dish and spread the lettuce in it. Season with a pinch of salt and chilli flakes. Cut the cheese into slices and place on top.

Bake at 180 ° C in a preheated oven for 5-10 minutes (alternatively for about 1 minute at maximum power in the microwave).

Cut open the pita bread and brush with a little butter. Warm up briefly in the toaster or oven. Place the lettuce and cheese mixture in the pita bread and top it with cress, fresh lettuce leaves or tomato notes as desired.

CLASSIC SMORES

Servings:6

INGREDIENTS

- 12 Pc Graham crackers or butter biscuits
- 3 Pk Hershey's milk chocolate or Swiss chocolate
- 12 Stg   Marshmallows

PREPARATION

Put the marshmallows on branches to grill them over the remaining embers on the grill or over an open campfire. (Attention: It is essential to pay attention to the choice of branches. Beech, willow and hazelnut wood are particularly suitable for this.) An alternative to branches would be a barbecue fork.

When the marshmallow is roasted, a piece of chocolate is placed on a biscuit, the marshmallow is placed on top and another biscuit is placed on top. Do the same for all 12 marshmallows.

Let the sandwiches cool down a bit and enjoy them while they are still warm.

CHEESE AND ARUGULA CORE SANDWICH

Servings:2

INGREDIENTS

- 10 G butter
- 6 Schb   Gruyères cheese
- 2 Pc   Seed bread, e.g. "Pagnol"
- 20 G arugula
- 0.25 Pc   Cucumber

PREPARATION

Halve the core bread lengthways and cut into sandwich-sized pieces.

Brush the base with butter, pour 3 slices of Gruyères cheese over each and cover with cucumber slices.

Pour rocket into the rolls, close with a bread cover and transport the sandwiches well wrapped to the office.

CHEESE AND CUCUMBER SANDWICH

Servings:1

INGREDIENTS

- 1 Pc   baguette
- 50 G Gruyères cheese
- 1 prize   pepper
- 0.5 Pc Cucumber
- 1 Tbsp   Mustard butter

PREPARATION

Cut the fresh baguette lengthways and brush with mustard butter.

Wash, slice and cover the cucumber.

Cut the cheese into slices and place on the cucumber pieces.

Pepper the cheese and cucumber sandwich, wrap up and enjoy.

HOT SANDWICH WITH HAM AND EGG

Servings:4

INGREDIENTS

- 8 Schb   thickly sliced toast
- 4 Pc   Eggs
- 300 G cooked, smoked ham, finely sliced
- 150 G cheese
- 1 Tbsp   oil
- 3 Tbsp   mustard
- 50 G soft butter

PREPARATION

Coat the toast slices with mustard on one side. Then fry 4 fried eggs in the oil. Divide the ham on 4 slices of toast, add an egg, the sliced cheese and a slice of toast each, so that 4 sandwiches are created.

Butter the outside of the sandwiches and fry them on both sides in a frying pan until golden brown.

QUICK SPRING SANDWICH

Servings:1

INGREDIENTS

- 20 G Garden cress, fresh
- 40 G Herbal cream cheese
- 4 Pc Lettuce leaves / or arugula
- 4 Pc Tomato slices
- 2 Pc whole-grain bread rolls

PREPARATION

Cut the whole grain bread crosswise.

Spread herbal cream cheese on the lower half of the rolls.

Spread the garden cress on the cream cheese layer.

Place lettuce leaves or rocket and tomato slices on top, close the top half of the roll and enjoy the sandwich.

CREAM CHEESE BAGUETTES WITH RADISHES

Servings:1

INGREDIENTS

- 1 Pc   Baguette rolls, large
- 2 Tbsp   cream cheese
- 3 Pc   radish
- 2 Bl   Salad, fresh
- 0.25 Pc   Cucumber

PREPARATION

Cut the baguette roll lengthways and brush with cream cheese.

Wash the radishes, cucumber and lettuce, drain and prepare if necessary. Cut the lettuce and radishes into fine slices and place on the cream cheese topping.

Place the lettuce leaves on the raw vegetables and seal the sandwich with the baguette top.

FETA AND BÜNDNERFLEISCH SANDWICH WITH ROCKET

Servings:2

INGREDIENTS

- 50 G Bündnerfleisch
- 10 G butter
- 30 G Feta sheep cheese
- 2 Schb cucumber
- 2 Pc Seed bread, e.g. "Pagnol"
- 20 G arugula

PREPARATION

Cut the core bread into sandwich-sized sections and create a lengthways to cover.

Brush the underside with butter. Place Bündnerfleisch on top, crumble the feta and stand on top.

Place the cucumber slices over the feta cheese and top the sandwich topping with rocket. Cover up, pack well and enjoy in the office!

EGG AND BAGUETTE SANDWICH

Servings:1

INGREDIENTS

- 1 Pc   Baguette, small
- 1 Pc   Hardboiled egg
- 3 Tbsp   low-fat quark
- 1 prize   paprika
- 0.25 Federation   Parsley, fresh
- 1 prize   pepper
- 2 Bl   Lettuce, green
- 1 prize   salt
- 0.25 Federation   Chives, fresh
- 1 shot Lemon juice

PREPARATION

Halve the fresh baguette lengthways.

Wash and chop the chives and parsley.

Finely chop the hard-boiled egg and mix with low-fat quark, lemon juice, chopped herbs and spices.

Cover the baguette with lettuce leaves and spread the quark and egg mixture on top. Enjoy it immediately or take it to the office for lunch.

BROCCOLI HAM BREAD SLICES

Servings:4

INGREDIENTS

- 530 G broccoli
- 1 Tbsp   butter
- 120 G Gruyère, grated
- 1 Pc   clove of garlic
- 1 prize   nutmeg
- 1 prize   pepper
- 8 Schb   Rye bread
- 1 Pc   Red onion
- 1 prize   salt
- 170 G Hollandaise sauce
- 120 G Cooked ham

PREPARATION

Wash the fresh broccoli, prepare and cut into florets. Cut the stalks of it into small pieces. Both are blanched in a pot with boiling salted water for about 4 minutes. Then pour off, rinse in cold water and drain well.

Then peel and finely chop the red onion and garlic. Then sauté both in a pan with a little butter for about 5 minutes. Then add the broccoli and cook for about 5 minutes. Season well with salt, pepper and nutmeg.

Dice the juicy ham and mix with the broccoli mixture in a bowl. Preheat the oven to 220 ° C. Place the bread slices on a baking sheet lined with baking paper and cover evenly with the broccoli mixture. Pour 1 tablespoon of hollandaise sauce over each and sprinkle with cheese.

Then bake the bread slices in the oven for about 5 minutes. Then serve hot immediately and enjoy.

WHOLE GRAIN TOAST

Servings:1

INGREDIENTS

- 4 Schb   Gouda cheese
- 4 Schb   Chicken breast (smoked)
- 1 Tbsp   Herbal cream cheese
- 4 Schb   paprika
- 4 Schb   radish

PREPARATION

Toast the toast to the desired color.

Brush with cream cheese, top with sausage and cheese and garnish with the vegetables.

BAGUETTE WITH STRIPS OF CHICKEN

Servings:4

INGREDIENTS

- 2 Stg Baguette breads
- 3 Pc   Basil, stalks
- 5 Tbsp   mayonnaise
- 2 Pk   Mozzarella
- 2 Tbsp   oil
- 1 prize   pepper
- 280 G Chicken breast fillet
- 1 prize   salt
- 2 Tbsp   mustard
- 2 Pc   tomatoes
- 2 TL Lemon juice
- 1 prize   sugar

PREPARATION

Cut the chicken breast into strips, then fry them with a little oil in a pan while turning for about 5 minutes. Then season with salt and pepper.

Wash and slice the tomatoes. Take the mozzarella out of the package and cut into slices in the same way. Rinse the basil and shake dry. Mix the mayonnaise with the mustard and lemon juice well and season well with salt, pepper and sugar.

Halve the baguette, cut open from above and unfold. First brush with a little mayonnaise, then fill with tomatoes, mozzarella, chicken strips and basil leaves. Drizzle with the remaining mayonnaise and serve.

WILD GARLIC AND CHEESE SAUCE

Servings:4

INGREDIENTS

- 70 G Wild garlic
- 220 ml   Bouillon (vegetables)
- 120 G cream cheese
- 2 Tbsp   oil
- 1 prize   pepper
- 100 ml   cream
- 1 prize   salt
- 1 Pc   lemon
- 1 Pc   onion

PREPARATION

First bring the bouillon to the boil in a saucepan.

Peel the onion and chop finely. Wash the fresh lemon with hot water, dry it and finely rub the peel. Then cut in half and squeeze out 1 tablespoon of lemon juice.

Sauté the onions in a deep pan with a little oil for about 5 minutes. Deglaze with the bouillon and stir in the cream and cream cheese. Bring the whole thing to the boil slowly while stirring.

Wash the fresh wild garlic, shake it dry and chop it finely. Put the chopped wild garlic with the lemon zest in the pan. Bring to the boil and season well with salt, pepper and lemon juice. Serve hot immediately.

EGGPLANT SANDWICHES

Servings:2

INGREDIENTS

- 2 Pc Eggplant
- 6 Tbsp   Flour
- 230 G Mozzarella
- 4 Tbsp   oil
- 1 prize   salt
- 10 Pc Anchovy fillets
- 1 Pc Tomato, big

PREPARATION

Wash the fresh eggplants and cut across into 10 slices.
The flour is mixed with salt in a deep plate. Then turn
the aubergine slices in it thoroughly.

Then fry the slices in a pan with a little oil on both sides for a few minutes. Then drain the slices on kitchen paper and dab off the oil.

Cut the fresh mozzarella into 10 slices. Wash the firm tomato, remove the stalk and cut into 5 slices. Place 1 tomato slice and 2 anchovy fillets and 1 mozzarella slice on each of 5 aubergine slices and cover with an aubergine slice.

Fry the eggplant sandwiches with a little oil in the pan again for about 3 minutes and turn until the cheese melts a little. Arrange and serve the sandwiches immediately.

APERITIF TOAST SQUARES

Servings:6

INGREDIENTS

- 20 G butter
- 2 Pc Pickles
- 100 G Salmon, fresh
- 170 G Toast Weggli
- 70 G Turkey breast
- 0.5 Pc onion

PREPARATION

Toast the toasted rolls for about 3-5 minutes at 200 degrees Celsius in the middle of the oven. Let something cool down.

Spread butter evenly on the toast rolls.

Halve the turkey breast slices, fold them to the corner and roll up full. Finely knead the pickles and place them as a decoration.

Separate the salmon into pieces with a fork and drape them on the toast rolls.

Finely cut the onion into rings and pour over the salmon rolls.

Arrange aperitif toast squares on a nice plate and serve with an aperitif.

CIABATTA PANINI

Servings:4

INGREDIENTS

- 1 Pc   aubergine
- 2 Tbsp   Basil, fresh
- 4 Pc   Ciabatta or other white bread
- 12 Bl Green lettuce leaves
- 500 G Mozzarella
- 2 Tbsp   olive oil
- 140 G Parma ham
- 2 Tbsp   Pesto, green
- 1 prize   pepper
- 1 prize   salt
- 7 Pc   Tomatoes, dried
- 2 Pc   Zucchini

PREPARATION

Drain the fresh mozzarella and cut into small cubes. Cut the ham and the dried tomatoes into fine strips. Rinse the fresh basil, shake dry and finely chop. Put all these ingredients in a bowl, season with salt and pepper and mix well.

Wash the fresh courgettes and aubergines, prepare and cut into thin slices. Put some oil in a pan and fry the courgette slices for about 3 minutes, fry the aubergines for about 7 minutes until they are soft. Season to taste with a little salt, pepper and pesto.

Halve the ciabatta rolls and fill with the mozzarella mixture, and cover the vegetable slices. Refine with lettuce leaves if you like. Drizzle with a little pesto. Cover the bread with the lid and serve.

AMERICAN DRESSING

Servings:1

INGREDIENTS

- 50 G Creme fraiche Cheese
- 170 G yogurt
- 50 G Ketchup
- 1 prize   parsley
- 1 prize   chives
- 1 TL mustard
- 2 TL Lemon juice
- 1 TL sugar

PREPARATION

Mix the creamy yogurt with the crème fraiche,
mustard, ketchup, lemon juice and sugar in a bowl.

Season well with chives, parsley, salt and pepper and place in the fridge until ready to serve.

DONER KEBAB

Servings:4

INGREDIENTS

- 400 g leg of lamb (or shoulder meat; alternatively also chicken or veal)
- 100 g bacon (from mutton)
- 500 g tomatoes
- beef broth
- 1 onion (red)
- 1/4 head lettuce (to taste)
- Cabbage (grated, to taste)
- 1/2 cucumber
- some hot peppersFor the marinade:
- 2 cloves of garlic
- 1/4 teaspoon salt
- 2 tbsp olive oil
- 1 teaspoon tomato paste

- 1/2 teaspoon paprika meal (Turkish)
- 1 pinch of pepper (black, ground)
- 1 pinch of new spices (ground)
- 1 pinch of cinnamon
- 1 pinch of cumin
- 1 pinch of thyme (dried, rubbed)
- For the yogurt sauce:
- 500 g yogurt (Turkish, 10% FiT)
- 3 cloves of garlic

PREPARATION

For the doner kebab, first finely puree the garlic with the salt in a mortar and mix with the other ingredients.

Cut the meat and fat into 3 cm cubes, mix with the marinade and leave to stand for 12 hours (preferably overnight). Put the meat and bacon on skewers, putting a piece of bacon every three meat cubes. Grill for 5-6 minutes, brushing with soup every now and then.

Mash the garlic with the salt in a mortar, stir into the yoghurt.

Cut the onion and tomatoes into slices. Cut the lettuce into strips. You may also want to leave some leaves whole. Halve the cucumber lengthways twice and then cut into slices.

Remove the grilled meat cubes from the skewer and cut them even smaller (into slices).

Halve the flatbread, cut a pocket into it. Pour the ingredients into the flatbread one after the other. Finally add the yogurt sauce to the doner kebab .

tip

If you want, you can also spice up the doner kebab . Depending on the taste, individual ingredients can also be left out or others added.

SAVORY SANDWICH CAKE

Servings:4

INGREDIENTS

- 14 slice (s) of toast bread
- 200 g ham
- 75 g garlic salami (or other strong whole sausage)
- 125 g Emmentaler (grated)
- 4 pickles
- Capers (at will)
- 3/4 teaspoon wasabi paste (or grated horseradish from the jar)
- 1 teaspoon Dijon mustard
- 1 cup of crème fraîche
- 1 packet of Gervais
- 150 g butter (room temperature)
- For the set:

- 175 g Gervais (natural; or crème fraîche)
- 1 bunch of chives
- salt
- pepper
- Olives
- Capers
- Pickle Guy
- Salami rolls

PREPARATION

For the savory sandwich cake, cut the ham and salami very finely or chop with a chopping knife. Finely chop the pickles and capers as well.

In a bowl, stir the butter at room temperature until foamy, mix well with the crème fraîche and Gervais. Mix with the chopped ingredients and grated cheese. Season with horseradish and Dijon mustard.

Cut away the crust of the toast (don't throw it away, dry it and grate it into crumbs). Line a not too large springform pan with a layer of bread and cut the slices as needed.

Brush with some filling compound, cover again with bread and repeat until everything is used up. Finish with a layer of bread. Press the bread on well, cover with cling film and leave to stand in a cool place for 1-2 hours.

In the meantime, finely chop the chives. Stir the Gervais, season with salt and pepper and stir in about half of the chives. Remove the cake from the springform pan and brush with the chives cream.

The savory sandwich layer places on the surface at the outer edge whim decorate with hard-boiled eggs, salami Rolls, capers, olives and / or Essiggurkerln. Scatter the rest of the chives over the middle and serve the sandwich cake.

tip

The savory sandwich cake is even easier with the appropriate step-by-step video instructions.

ENGLISH AFTERNOON TEA SANDWICHES

Servings:8

INGREDIENTS

- 16 slice (s) of wholemeal toast
- 2 eggs
- 2 sprig (s) of basil
- 2 sprig (s) of dill
- 1/2 piece of cucumber
- 150 g cream cheese
- Lemon juice (some)
- salt
- Pepper (from the mill)
- 30 g pistachios (chopped)
- 100 g mayonnaise

PREPARATION

For the English afternoon tea sandwiches, remove the crust from all the toast slices. Boil the eggs hard, quench them well, peel and chop them up.

Rinse the basil and dill, shake dry, pluck and finely chop each. Wash the cucumber and thinly slice or slice it.

Mix the dill with the cream cheese and season with lemon juice, salt and pepper. Spread on 8 slices of toast and cover 4 slices with the cucumber.

Cover with the remaining 4 coated discs (coated side facing down) and press down lightly.

Mix the eggs with the basil, pistachios and mayonnaise and season with lemon juice, salt and pepper.

Spread on 4 slices of toast and cover with the remaining slices.

Halve all slices diagonally and serve the English afternoon tea sandwiches.

Tip

It is best to use homemade mayonnaise for English afternoon tea sandwiches.

In our basic mayonnaise recipe, we will show you how you can easily make mayonnaise yourself .

PARTY PRETZEL

Servings:10

INGREDIENTS

- Vegetable mayonnaise (for brushing)
- For the dough:
- 1 1/4 kg of flour
- 3 tbsp salt
- 4 tbsp olive oil
- 1 cube of yeast (fresh)
- 800 ml water (warm)
- To sprinkle:
- sesame oil
- Poppy For covering:
- sausage
- cheese

- salad
- vegetables
- fishes
- Eggs

PREPARATION

For the party pretzel , prepare a smooth yeast dough the evening before using flour, salt, olive oil, yeast and water and leave to rise in the refrigerator overnight. Shape the pretzel, sprinkle with sesame seeds, poppy seeds and cheese and let rise on the baking sheet until the volume has doubled.

Bake in a preheated oven at 250 degrees for 15-20 minutes. Spray with water, cover with a cloth and allow to cool. Halve , brush with vegetable mayonnaise and top the party pretzel with salad, sausage or fish, cheese, eggs and vegetables, as you like.

HUNTERBUN

Servings:1

INGREDIENTS

- 1 piece sandwich
- 100 g butter
- 100 g cream cheese
- 1 tbsp mustard
- 1 tbsp mayonnaise
- 80 g Gouda
- 60 g press ham
- 2 pieces of pickled gherkins
- 50 g salami
- 2 eggs (hard-boiled)
- salt
- parsley
- pepper

PREPARATION

For the hunter's awakening, cut one end of the sandwich and scoop out the bread with a spoon. Pluck the bread mixture into small pieces and set aside.

Mix the butter with cream cheese, mustard and mayonnaise until creamy and season with salt and pepper. Add parsley. Work in the bread mixture. Cut the Gouda, ham, salami, pickles and eggs into small pieces and mix well with the butter and bread mixture.

Pour the mixture into the sandwich and wrap it in cling film and let it rest in the refrigerator for a few hours.

Cut the Jägerwecken into slices and serve.

PORK FILLET IN FLATBREAD WITH POINTED CABBAGE AND GARLIC MAYONNAISE

Servings:4

INGREDIENTS

- 600 g pork fillet
- Oil (for frying)
- Butter (for frying)
- salt
- Pepper (from the mill)
- For the stain:
- 100 g rose hip jam
- 60 ml malt beer
- 4 sprigs of thyme
- 1 sprig (s) of rosemary

- 3 cloves of garlic (large; peeled)
- 2 allspice grainsFor the herb:
- 300 g pointed cabbage
- 2 tbsp granulated sugar
- 1 lemon (untreated; juice and zest)
- salt
- Pepper (from the mill)
- 1 pinch of caraway seeds (whole)
- 3 tbsp olive oilFor the flatbread:
- 500 g flour (smooth)
- 330 ml water (lukewarm)
- 3 tbsp olive oil
- 1 package dry yeast
- 1 teaspoon salt
- 1 teaspoon marjoram For the mayonnaise:
- 2 egg yolks
- 3 cloves of garlic (large)
- 100 ml of sunflower oil
- 1 squirt of lemon juice
- 1 pinch of salt
- 1 pinch of pepper (from the mill)

PREPARATION

For the flatbread, first knead all the ingredients into a smooth dough, divide into 4 pieces and shape into balls with circular movements. Cover and let rest for about 20 minutes.

Preheat the oven to 220 ° C top / bottom heat. Carefully press the dough balls flat, brush them with lukewarm water and bake them in the preheated oven for 5 minutes at 220 ° C, then for a further 10-12 minutes at 180 ° C. Let cool down.

The cabbage cut into very fine strips or planing. Knead well with salt, sugar, lemon juice and zest, caraway seeds, pepper and olive oil. Let it steep for about 15 minutes.

Mix all the stain ingredients in a mortar or a chopper to a fine paste.

The pork tenderloin zuputzen. Sear the meat on all sides in a little oil in a preheated pan. Then reduce the heat and coat the meat all around with the stain. Add the butter to the pan and cook the fillet over low heat for approx. 8-10 minutes, turning and brushing with the stain.

Set the pan aside and let the meat simmer for another 5 minutes. Then cut the pork fillet into thin slices.

Mix the gravy with the rest of the stain and season with salt and pepper.

In a tall vessel made of egg yolks, lemon juice and the peeled garlic cloves, mix a paste with a hand blender, mix in the oil in a thin stream and season the mayonnaise with salt and pepper.

Halve the bread horizontally, brush with the mayonnaise, spread the pointed cabbage and the sliced pork fillet on top and serve garnished with lettuce.

VIP CLUB SANDWICH

Servings:2

INGREDIENTS

- 6 Schb   loaf
- 4 Tbsp   KUNER mayonnaise 25% fat
- 4 Schb   Chicken breast (cooked)
- 1 kpf Iceberg lettuce
- 2 Pc   Tomato (sliced)
- 0.5 Pc Cucumber (sliced)
- 4 Schb   Bacon (crispy)

PREPARATION

Toast the bread. Put KUNER mayonnaise on 2 slices of
the toasted bread.

Cover with a little lettuce, tomatoes, cucumber and a slice of chicken breast. Place another slice of bread on top of the chicken and cover with a little mayonnaise.

Place the lettuce, tomato, cucumber and the crispy bacon on the bread. Finally, place the second slice of toast on top of the bacon.

Halve the sandwiches diagonally and secure with cocktail skewers. Serve with raw vegetables.

CUCUMBER SANDWICH

Servings:2

INGREDIENTS

- 4 Schb   Toast (debarked)
- 1 Pc   Cucumber (small)
- 1 prize   salt
- 2 Tbsp   butter
- 1 Tbsp   Lemon juice
- 1 prize   Pepper White)

PREPARATION

Peel, halve and core the cucumber. Thinly slice or slice the cucumber.

Mix the cucumber slices with salt, pepper and lemon juice and leave to marinate for 5 minutes, then drain well in a sieve.

Brush the toast slices with butter on one side and cover with the cucumber slices, possibly add a little salt / pepper.

Cut both sandwiches one or two times diagonally and serve.

SANDWICH LASAGNA

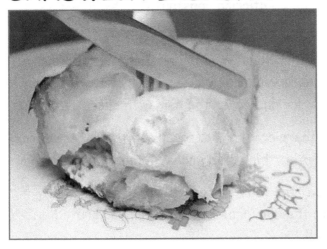

Servings:4

INGREDIENTS

- 10 Pc Slices of toast
- 1 Pc   onion
- 1 shot Oil for the pan
- 5 Tbsp   Tomato sauce
- 3 Tbsp   sour cream
- 150 G Boiled ham, sliced
- 200 G Sliced cheese
- 100 G Mozzarella into pieces
- 100   GCheese, grated

PREPARATION

For our sandwich lasagne, first peel the onion, chop it
finely and fry it briefly in a pan with a little oil.

Then add the tomato sauce and the sour cream and simmer briefly - stirring constantly.

Now line the bottom of a baking dish with slices of toast (sandwich toast) and brush the slices of toast with the sauce you made earlier. Place a layer of ham over the sauce and cover the ham with slices of cheese.

Spread a few pieces of mozzarella on the cheese slices and cover everything with slices of toasted bread.

Finally, coat the toast slices with the sauce again, distribute the ham, mozzarella pieces and grated cheese well.

Now bake the casserole dish for about 15 minutes in the preheated oven (top / bottom heat) at 220 degrees.

AVOCADO SANDWICH

Servings: 2

INGREDIENTS

- 1 Tbsp   Ayvar
- 1 Tbsp   Tomato paste
- 2 TL Lemon juice
- 1 Pc Avocado (ripe)
- 1 Pc Onion (red)
- 2 Schb   Gouda cheese
- 1 Pc baguette
- 1 prize   pepper
- 1 prize   salt

PREPARATION

Preheat the oven to 200 °. Meanwhile stir together
Ayvar, tomato paste and 1 teaspoon lemon juice. Season
well with salt and pepper.

Peel the avocado and cut into strips. After peeling, cut the onion into fine rings and halve the cheese.

Cut the baguette into slices and place on a baking sheet, brush with the cream, place the avocado and onion rings on top and cover with the cheese. Finally season with salt and pepper and bake in the oven for 5 minutes.

VEGETABLE SANDWICH

Servings:4

INGREDIENTS

- 8 Schb toast
- 2 Pc tomatoes
- 1 Pc onion
- 50 G Parmesan
- 0.5 Pc Lettuce
- 3 Pc Eggs
- 40 G butter

PREPARATION

Hard boil eggs, quench, peel and cut into slices.

Clean the lettuce, wash, pat dry and pluck into bite-sized pieces. Peel the onion. Wash tomatoes. Dice the onion and tomatoes. Slice the parmesan.

Toast slices of toast lightly. Let cool and brush with the butter.

Cover four slices of toast with the prepared ingredients and pepper. Cover with the remaining toast slices. Press lightly together and cut once diagonally.

LEMON CHICKEN SANDWICH

Servings: 2

INGREDIENTS

- 2 Pc Chicken breasts
- 2 Tbsp   Lemon juice
- 2 Tbsp   Flour
- 0.5 Tbsp   crushed fennel seeds
- 2 Tbsp   olive oil
- 1 Pc paprika
- 1 Federation arugula
- 8 Schb   Sandwich bread
- 1 prize pepper
- 1 prize   salt

PREPARATION

Flatten the chicken breasts (halved, boneless) and marinate with lemon juice for at least 20 minutes.

Mix the fennel, flour, salt and pepper. Drain the chicken and roll in it.

Fry the chicken in the oil for about 20 minutes. Take out of the pan.

Cut the paprika into strips, fry them with a little oil and add the lemon juice to the marinade until it has evaporated completely.

Toast sandwich bread, cut the chicken into slices and prepare sandwiches from the toasts, peppers and fillets.

CUCUMBER SANDWICH WITH LEMON BUTTER

Servings:4

INGREDIENTS

- 6 Tbsp butter
- 1 prize   pepper
- 1 Pc   Cucumber
- 1 prize   salt
- 12 Schb White bread
- 1 Pc   lemon
- 1 Tbsp   Lemon juice
- 1 Pa   Lettuce leaves
- 0.5 Pc paprika
- 1 prize   sugar

PREPARATION

Mix the butter with the grated lemon zest and lemon juice in a small bowl.

Spread a thin layer of butter on each slice of bread. Cover half of the slices with a thin layer of cucumber slices, lettuce leaves and paprika cut into strips.

Sprinkle lightly with sugar and pepper. Place the other buttered bread slices on top.

Trim the edges and cut each sandwich into 4 triangles.

AMERICAN STEAK TOAST

Servings:4

INGREDIENTS

- 4 Pc   Lettuce leaves
- 4 Pc   Tomato slices
- 400 G   pork tenderloin
- 4 Tbsp   Cocktail sauce
- 4 Schb   Cheese (spicy)
- 1 Tbsp   Clarified butter
- 1 prize   pepper
- 1 prize   salt

PREPARATION

For the American steak toasts, first wash the lettuce leaves thoroughly and shake dry. Also preheat the oven (200 ° grill function).

Now fry the pork fillet all around in hot clarified butter, season with salt and pepper and roast for 10 minutes while turning until the end. Then cut the pork tenderloin into slices.

Place a slice of cheese on the toast in the toaster and a slice of cheese on each of the steaks and place in the oven briefly at 200 ° C.

In the meantime, smear the cocktail sauce on the slices of toast and then place a lettuce leaf and a tomato slice on top. Only now do the steak slices with the slightly melted cheese come on. Bon appetit!

WHOLE GRAIN HEALTHY SANDWICH

Servings: 2

INGREDIENTS

- 4 Schb   Whole grain bread
- 1 Pc   avocado
- 4 Tbsp   cottage cheese
- 1 Tbsp   Chopped coriander
- 2 Spr Lemon juice
- 3 prize   pepper
- 3 prize   salt

PREPARATION

Halve the avocado, remove the stone and lift the pulp out of the skin. Cut the avocado into thin wedges and drizzle with a little lemon juice.

Spread 1 tablespoon of cottage cheese on two whole meal breads, then spread the avocado slices on top. Season with a strong pinch of salt and pepper and spread the rest of the cottage cheese on top. Cover with the blank slice of bread and enjoy.

ITALIAN SANDWICHES

Servings:4

INGREDIENTS

- 2 Tbsp   olive oil
- 1 Pc   Onion (finely chopped)
- 1 Pc   Garlic (finely chopped)
- 1 Pc   Bell pepper (red, finely chopped)
- 200 G Minced beef
- 125 ml   red wine
- 2 Tbsp   Tomato paste
- 4 Pc   ciabatta
- 75 G Mozzarella
- 2 Tbsp   Basil leaves
- 1 prize   pepper
- 1 prize   salt

PREPARATION

Heat the oil in a larger saucepan and fry the onions, garlic, bell peppers and mushrooms over medium heat. keep stirring. After 5 minutes the minced meat is added and browned while stirring constantly.

Then add wine, tomato paste and salt and pepper and simmer for another 10 minutes.

In the meantime, cut open the ciabatta, brush the cut surface with oil and place the undersides on a large piece of aluminum foil. Now distribute the meat mixture evenly on top.

Cut the cheese into slices and distribute on the rolls. Now sprinkle with the basil and place the tops on top. Either serve immediately or let it steep for about an hour.

HAM SANDWICH

Servings:2

INGREDIENTS

- 1 Tbsp oil
- 8 Schb ham
- 3 Schb toast
- 2 Pc tomatoes
- 1 TL butter
- 4 Bl salad
- 1 prize pepper
- 1 prize salt

PREPARATION

Wash the lettuce and drain well. Wash tomatoes, cut into slices and season.

Brown the toast slices in the toaster and cut them diagonally. Brush four toast corners with butter.

Fry half of the ham slices in a pan with a little oil. Cover two toast corners with lettuce, one slice each of fried and fresh ham and tomato slices.

Place two more toast corners on top and cover them in the same way. Finish with toast corners and secure with toothpicks.

CLUB SANDWICH

Servings:4

INGREDIENTS

- 4 Pc Turkey schnitzel
- 8 Pc toast
- 1 Pc tomatoes
- 1 Pc salad
- 2 Pc onion
- 4 Schb   cheese

PREPARATION

For the club sandwich, the turkey schnitzel is seasoned with salt, pepper and a little chili. Fry the meat on both sides in a pan and top with the cheese - let it simmer in the pan until the cheese has melted.

Cut the tomatoes into slices and cut the lettuce very small. Also cut the onions into small pieces and fry them in a pan until golden brown.

Toast the toast in the toaster until golden brown. Cover the finished toast with the cut lettuce and a slice of the tomato. Put the meat and the onions on the toast and finally put a second toast as a lid on the finished dish.

You can also make a yogurt sauce for serving.

GRILLED CHEESE SANDWICH

Servings:2

INGREDIENTS

- 2 Schb   Whole grain bread
- 200 G Grilled cheese
- 2 Pc Lettuce
- 0.5 Pc tomatoes
- 1 prize   salt
- 1 prize   pepper
- 1 shot oil

PREPARATION

First grill the bread slices in the toaster until golden brown and briefly fry the grilled cheese with a little oil in the pan on both sides.

Wash the crispy lettuce and tomato and cut the tomato into slices.

Then cover the grilled bread slices with the lettuce leaves, the tomatoes and the lightly seared grilled cheese and season with salt and pepper as desired.

SHEEP CHEESE SANDWICH

Servings:2

INGREDIENTS

- 1 Pc   Eggplant (small)
- 1 prize   salt
- 0.25 Federation   Rocket (approx. 20 g)
- 1 Pc   tomato
- 3 TL olive oil
- 4   Schb   Whole meal spelled bread
- 1 prize   pepper
- 40 G Sheep cheese

PREPARATION

First wash the aubergines thoroughly, cut off the ends
and then cut lengthways into approx. 8 thin slices. Place
the slices side by side on kitchen paper, lightly salt and
let steep for about 5 minutes.

In the meantime, wash the rocket, shake it dry and remove the coarse stalks. Wash the tomato and pat dry. Then cut out the stem end and cut the tomato like the eggplant into 8 thin slices. Now heat a teaspoon of olive oil in a non-stick pan and toast the bread slices over medium heat on each side for about 3 minutes until golden brown. Take out and let cool.

Now pat the aubergines dry with kitchen paper. Heat the olive oil again in the non-stick pan, fry 4 aubergine slices over medium heat for about 3 minutes until golden brown. Season with pepper. Fry the rest of the aubergines in the rest of the oil. Take out, place on a plate and let cool down.

Top two slices of toasted bread with half of the eggplant, rocket and tomato each. Then sprinkle some pepper over it.

Pat the sheep cheese dry. And cut four slices down. They are then placed on the sandwiches and sprinkled with pepper again. Place the remaining two slices of bread on top as a lid and press lightly. Finished!

AVOCADO SANDWICH CREAM

Servings:4

INGREDIENTS

- 2 Pc avocado
- 50 G Mayonnaise (vegan)
- 2 Pc Limes
- 1 prize salt
- 1 prize pepper

PREPARATION

Halve and core the avocado. Remove the pulp with a spoon and place in a bowl.

Add the lime juice and mayonnaise and blend with the hand blender until you have a homogeneous mixture.

Season with salt and pepper to taste.

BANANA SANDWICH

Servings:2

INGREDIENTS

- 4 Schb   Toast bread, great
- 1 Pc   banana
- 2 Tbsp   apricot jam
- 2 Tbsp   white almond butter

PREPARATION

First brush 2 toasted breads with jam, then with white almond butter.

Then cut the bananas into slices and place them on toast.

Close, cut diagonally and serve.

CAMEMBERT SANDWICH

Servings:2

INGREDIENTS

- 1 Pc ciabatta
- 2 Pc Camembert
- 1 Pc orange

PREPARATION

Cut open the ciabatta and place on the baking sheet together with the camembert. Bake in the oven for 5 minutes at 200 ° C.

Meanwhile, peel the orange and remove the white spots with a sharp knife. Then cut the orange into slices.

Cut the warm camembert into slices, place on the ciabatta and top with orange slices.

Serve warm and enjoy.

CUCUMBER SANDWICH

Servings:2

INGREDIENTS

- 4 Schb   Whole grain toast
- 3 Tbsp   cream cheese
- 120 G cucumber
- 1 prize   pepper
- 1 prize salt

PREPARATION

Lay the loaves on top of each other and cut off the rind, spread evenly with cream cheese. Wash the cucumber and cut into thin slices, spread on the toast.

Season with salt and pepper and fold 2 loaves of bread together. Halve the bread diagonally and leave to taste.

SNACK SANDWICH

Servings:4

INGREDIENTS

- 100 G ham
- 8 Pc toast
- 2 Pc tomatoes
- 50 G Parmesan
- 3 Pc Eggs
- 40 G butter
- 4 Bl salad
- 1 prize   pepper

PREPARATION

Hard boil eggs, quench, peel and cut into slices. Cut ham into strips. Coarsely grate the parmesan.

Clean the lettuce, wash, pat dry and pluck into bite-sized pieces. Wash and dice tomatoes. Slice the parmesan.

Toast slices of toast lightly. Let cool and brush with the butter.

Cover four slices of toast with the prepared ingredients and pepper. Cover with the remaining toast slices. Press lightly together and cut once diagonally.

WHOLE GRAIN BREAD WITH CURD CHEESE

Servings:1

INGREDIENTS

- 1 Schb   Whole grain bread
- 1 Tbsp   Potting
- 1 prize   Seasoned Salt
- 1 TL   Cut chives
- 0.5 prize   Flea seeds

PREPARATION

Spread the whole meal bread with curd cheese and season with herbal salt to taste. Sprinkle the chopped chives and the psyllium on the pot.

FLANK STEAK SANDWICH

Servings: 2

INGREDIENTS

- 2 Pc   Ciabatta or baguette
- 0.5 Pc Iceberg lettuce

For the flank steak

- 600 G Flank steak
- 2 Pc Garlic cloves
- 3 Tbsp   Rapeseed oil
- 2 Tbsp   soy sauce
- 1 TL Paprika powder
- 1 prize   salt
- 1 prize   pepper
- 1 prize   pimento
- for the cream
- 1 Pc   green jalapeño chilli

- 10 G chives
- 200 G cream cheese
- 1 prize   salt
- 1 prize   pepper

for the sauce

- 0.5 Pc Mango, very ripe
- 1 TL   Apple Cider Vinegar
- 1 Tbsp   olive oil
- 2 Tbsp   Acacia honey

PREPARATION

For the marinade, first peel and finely chop the garlic, then mix with the rapeseed oil, soy sauce, paprika and allspice and season with a little pepper.

Place the flank steak in the mixture and marinate for at least 30 minutes.

In the meantime, roughly cut the iceberg lettuce, peel and slice the avocado and red onions and set aside.

For the cream, finely chop the jalapeño chilli and chives, mix with the cream cheese and season with salt and pepper.

For the sauce, peel the mango and remove the pulp from the core. Using a hand blender, process apple cider vinegar, olive oil and acacia honey into a smooth sauce.

Then cut the bread in half lengthways. Remove the steak from the marinade, pat dry and season with a little salt.

Then prepare the grill for direct heat at 250 ° C. Place the steak directly on the grillage and fry over direct heat for 2-3 minutes on each side.

Place the steak over the indirect heat and let it rest until it has reached the desired core temperature.

Finally, remove the steak from the grill and let it rest for another 5 minutes in a warm place. Toast the bread for about 1 minute on each side.

Finally, finely chop the meat, spread the cream on the bread, cover with the salad, pieces of avocado, onion and meat and enjoy with the sauce.

SHORTBREAD SANDWICH

Servings:4

INGREDIENTS

- 8 Pc shortbread
- 4 Tbsp   Mövenpick vanilla
- 1 Tbsp   Almonds (roasted, chopped)

PREPARATION

Let the vanilla ice cream thaw a little, then mix with the chopped roasted almonds.

Spread one tablespoon each on a shortbread biscuit and put a second butter on it, squeeze it a little hard and freeze it again for 2 hours (wrapped in cling film, you can leave it frozen for a longer time and "snack away" if necessary)

CONCLUSION

This is about a dish that is also healthy. Mushrooms

with shrimps, grilled fish with lettuce, zucchini cream,

grilled or baked chicken fillet with spices, boiled eggs

with tuna, etc. The combination of proteins with

vegetables is back at night. For dessert, you can have a

low-fat yogurt.

Sometimes you can alternate meals with dinner . So if

you leave the sandwich for the night, you can enjoy

pasta or potatoes with fish and meat for lunch, as

mentioned earlier. Of course, without forgetting a good

salad or a good vegetable dish.

It is true that it does not impose quantities and that it

is being questioned by many and many as a definitive

and wholesome method. But keeping it on for a certain

amount of time, alternating with these healthier dishes,

it helps us in those moments when work prevents us

from eating the way we want.